Japanese Traditional Soup

Would You Prefer Dashi Soup or Miso Soup?

By

Jennifer Jones

© 2019 Jennifer Jones, All Rights Reserved.

License Notices

The book, hereunto known as "The Book" shall not be copied or reproduced in any way without the express permission of the "The Author". "The Book" is licensed for single use and is not transferable. If you are in possession of an illegal download of "The Book", delete your version and purchase a new one.

The opinions, suggestions, directions and guidelines mentioned in "The Book" are strictly for informational use. The Author has gone to great lengths to ensure authenticity, but accepts no liability for any commercial or personal damage incurred by misinterpretation of "The Book". The Reader assumes all risk when following the content of the "The Book".

Get Your Daily Deals Here!

Thanks for buying my book! As a special offer, you are now eligible for free books when you sign up below. All you need to do is fill in your email address and offers will be emailed to you on a daily basis for free and discounted books. To make sure you never miss one of these unique offers, a reminder email will be sent to you a few days before the offer expires. You don't have to do a thing! Subscribe now in the box below and start receiving your thank you gift!

https://Jennifer-Jones.gr8.com

Table of Contents

Homemade Japanese Soup Recipes 7

    Recipe 1: Clam Miso Soup 8

    Recipe 2: Seared King Oyster Mushroom Miso Soup .. 10

    Recipe 3: Pulled Pork Miso Soup 13

    Recipe 4: Classic Miso Soup 15

    Recipe 5: Coconut Milk Miso Soup 17

    Recipe 6: Kale Miso Soup 19

    Recipe 7: Butternut Squash & Quinoa Miso Soup 21

    Recipe 8: Chicken Ramen Miso Soup 23

    Recipe 9: Swiss Chard Miso Soup 26

    Recipe 10: Sweet Potato Miso Soup 28

    Recipe 11: Black Bean & Tofu Miso Soup 30

    Recipe 12: Bacon & Onion Miso Soup 32

    Recipe 13: Cabbage & Tomato Miso Soup 34

Recipe 14: Beefy Miso Soup.. 36

Recipe 15: Shimeji & Bean Sprout Miso Soup............. 38

Recipe 16: Salmon Miso Soup....................................... 40

Recipe 17: Sweet Potato Noodle & Broccoli Miso Soup
.... 43

Recipe 18: Soy Milk Miso Soup 45

Recipe 19: Zoodle Miso Soup.. 47

Recipe 20: Shrimp Miso Soup 49

Recipe 21: Beef Udon Miso Soup.................................. 52

Recipe 22: Collard Green Miso Soup 54

Recipe 23: Shrimp & Lobster Miso Soup 56

Recipe 24: Shitake Mushroom Miso Soup.................... 58

Recipe 25: Salmon & Green Bean Miso Soup.............. 60

Recipe 26: Turmeric Miso Soup 62

Recipe 27: Adzuki Bean & Vegetable Miso Soup........ 65

Recipe 28: Shrimp & Broccoli Miso Soup 67

Recipe 29: Chorizo Miso Soup 69

Recipe 30: Lobster Miso Soup 71

About the Author 74

Author's Afterthoughts 76

Homemade Japanese Soup Recipes

Recipe 1: Clam Miso Soup

If you love mollusks then this soup is a must try.

Yield: 4

Preparation Time: 15 minutes

Ingredient List:

- Water (4 cups)
- Clams (1 lb., Asari)
- Shiro Miso (3 tablespoons, paste)
- Dark Miso (1 tablespoon, paste)
- Watercress Leaves (½ Cup)
- Garlic (2 cloves, minced)

Instructions:

1. Set your dashi on in a saucepan over high heat and allow to come to a boil.

2. Once it begins to boil, reduce to a low heat, and add in your miso paste then stir until your miso dissolve.

3. Add in your remaining ingredients, except watercress, and allow to cook for another 5 minutes.

4. Top with your watercress leaves, serve, and enjoy.

Recipe 2: Seared King Oyster Mushroom Miso Soup

This soup has a rich beef and mushroom broth.

Yield: 3

Preparation Time: 1 hr.

Ingredient List:

- Onion, large, diced (1)
- Carrots, diced (2)
- Celery, diced (3)
- Garlic, finely chopped (4 cloves)
- Kosher salt (1 teaspoon)
- Pepper (½ teaspoons)
- Green Bell Peppers (½ cup, sliced)
- Beef Short Ribs (1/s lbs., braised, chopped)
- Dashi (6 cups)
- Light Miso (2 teaspoons)
- Seared King Oyster Mushrooms (1 lb., chopped)
- Ramen Noodles (½ lb.)

HHHHHHHHHHHHHHHHHHHHHHHHHHHHHHHH

Instructions:

1. Prepare carrots, celery and onions for cooking in a saucepan for 5-7 minutes over medium heat. Add your salt, pepper, bell pepper and garlic, and continue to cook for an additional minute.

2. Add dashi and miso before bringing to a boil.

3. Once it begins to boil, stir in your remaining ingredients, and cook for approximately 5 minutes until mushrooms are tender.

4. Serve and enjoy!

Recipe 3: Pulled Pork Miso Soup

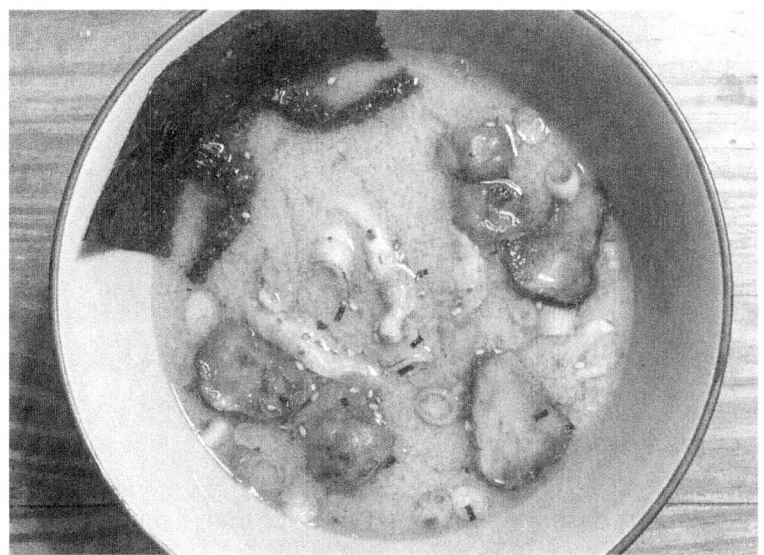

In this recipe it's all about the broth, but the chunks of pork make it even better.

Yield: 4

Preparation Time: 15 minutes

Ingredient List:

- Dashi (4 cups)
- Pork (1 cup., cooked, pulled)
- Miso (3 tablespoons, yellow, paste)
- Green Onions (½ cup, finely chopped)
- Garlic (2 cloves, minced)
- Soft Boiled Egg (2, halved)

HHHHHHHHHHHHHHHHHHHHHHHHHHHHHHHH

Instructions:

1. Set your dashi on in a saucepan over high heat and allow to come to a boil.

2. Once it begins to boil, reduce to a low heat, and add in your miso paste then stir until your miso dissolve.

3. Add in your remaining ingredients, except eggs, and allow to cook for another 5 minutes.

4. Top with your eggs, serve, and enjoy.

Recipe 4: Classic Miso Soup

Here is an easy recipe for a basic Miso Soup, similar to the one you would have at in a Japanese breakfast.

Yield: 5

Preparation Time: 15 minutes

Ingredient List:

- Dashi (4 cups)
- Tofu (1 lb., extra firm)
- Miso (5 tablespoons, paste)
- Green Onions (2 stalks, finely chopped)

HHHHHHHHHHHHHHHHHHHHHHHHHHHHHHHHHH

Instructions:

1. Set your dashi on in a saucepan over high heat and allow to come to a boil.

2. While that goes, cut your tofu into ½ inch cubes and add to your dashi pot.

3. Once it begins to boil, reduce to a low heat, and add in your miso paste then stir until your miso dissolve.

4. From this point on you will need to monitor the pot as you do not want your miso paste to boil or reduce as it already has a strong flavor.

5. Add in your onions, and remove from the flame.

6. Serve, and enjoy.

Recipe 5: Coconut Milk Miso Soup

Get the rich taste of coconut milk with the seasoned flavor of miso in this one bowl of soup.

Yield: 5

Preparation Time: 15 minutes

Ingredient List:

- Dashi (2 cups)
- Soy Milk (2 cups)
- Miso (5 tablespoons, white, paste)
- Mixed Vegetables (1 can, drained and rinsed)

HHHHHHHHHHHHHHHHHHHHHHHHHHHHHHHHH

Instructions:

1. Set your dashi, and coconut milk on in a saucepan over high heat and allow to come to a boil.

2. As soon as it begins to boil, reduce to a low heat, and add in your miso paste then stir until your miso dissolve.

3. Add in your vegetables, and allow to cook for about 4 more minutes before removing from the flame.

4. Serve, and enjoy.

Recipe 6: Kale Miso Soup

For a simple, healthy version of a classic miso soup, give this recipe a go.

Yield: 4

Preparation Time: 15 minutes

Ingredient List:

- Dashi (4 cups)
- Kale (½ cup., chopped)
- Miso (3 tablespoons, yellow, paste)
- Green Onions (½ cup, finely chopped)
- Garlic (2 cloves, minced)

Instructions:

1. Set your dashi on in a saucepan over high heat and allow to come to a boil.

2. Once it begins to boil, reduce to a low heat, and add in your miso paste then stir until your miso dissolve.

3. From this point on you will need to monitor the pot as you do not want your miso paste to boil or reduce as it already has a strong flavor.

4. Add in your remaining ingredients, and allow to cook for another 5 minutes.

5. Serve, and enjoy.

Recipe 7: Butternut Squash & Quinoa Miso Soup

This soup can be enjoyed at any time throughout the day.

Yield: 4

Preparation Time: 15 minutes

Ingredient List:

- Dashi (4 cups)
- Butternut Squash (1 lb., peeled, cubed)
- Quinoa (1 cup., cooked)
- Spinach (½ cup)
- Miso (3 tablespoons, yellow, paste)
- Garlic (2 cloves, minced)

HHHHHHHHHHHHHHHHHHHHHHHHHHHHHHHHH

Instructions:

1. Set your dashi, and squash on in a saucepan over high heat and allow sweet potatoes to become fork tender.

2. Once your potatoes are fork tender, reduce to a low heat, and add in your tofu, and miso paste then stir until your miso dissolve.

3. Add in your remaining ingredients, and allow to cook for another 5 minutes.

4. Serve, and enjoy.

Recipe 8: Chicken Ramen Miso Soup

If you love ramen you will love this recipe. It uses chicken instead of pork for all the chicken lovers.

Yield: 3

Preparation Time: 1 hr.

Ingredient List:

- Onion, large, diced (1)
- Carrots, diced (2)
- Celery, diced (3)
- Garlic, finely chopped (4 cloves)
- Kosher salt (1 teaspoon)
- Pepper (½ teaspoons)
- Cinnamon (2 teaspoons)
- Dashi (6 cups)
- Light Miso (2 teaspoons)
- Chicken breasts (1 lb.)
- Spinach (1 bag)
- Ramen Noodles (½ lb.)

HHHHHHHHHHHHHHHHHHHHHHHHHHHHHHHHH

Instructions:

1. Prepare carrots, celery and onions for cooking in a saucepan for 5-7 minutes over medium heat. Add your salt, pepper, cinnamon and garlic, and continue to cook for an additional minute.

2. Add dashi and miso before bringing to a boil.

3. Now add whole chicken breasts (raw), and simmer. Continue for 10-12 minutes. Occasionally remove a chicken breast and cut it, to see if it is cooked.

4. When the chicken is cooked thoroughly, relocate it to a cutting board for cooling.

5. When the chicken is cool enough to be handled, shred it, then add it back into the vegetable broth.

6. Stir in ramen noodles, and spinach to cook for approximately 5 minutes until spinach is tender.

7. Serve and enjoy!

Recipe 9: Swiss Chard Miso Soup

Spin your swiss chard into a delicious bowl of soup.

Yield: 4

Preparation Time: 15 minutes

Ingredient List:

- Dashi (4 cups)
- Swiss Chard (½ cup., chopped)
- Miso (3 tablespoons, yellow, paste)
- Green Onions (½ cup, finely chopped)
- Garlic (2 cloves, minced)

HHHHHHHHHHHHHHHHHHHHHHHHHHHHHHH

Instructions:

1. Set your dashi on in a saucepan over high heat and allow to come to a boil.

2. Once it begins to boil, reduce to a low heat, and add in your miso paste then stir until your miso dissolve.

3. From this point on you will need to monitor the pot as you do not want your miso paste to boil or reduce as it already has a strong flavor.

4. Add in your remaining ingredients, and allow to cook for another 5 minutes.

5. Serve, and enjoy.

Recipe 10: Sweet Potato Miso Soup

This miso soup is healthy, and delicious.

Yield: 4

Preparation Time: 15 minutes

Ingredient List:

- Dashi (4 cups)
- Tofu (1 lb., extra firm, cubed)
- Sweet Potato (1 cup., peeled, diced)
- Spinach (½ cup)
- Miso (3 tablespoons, yellow, paste)
- Green Onions (½ cup, finely chopped)
- Garlic (2 cloves, minced)

HHHHHHHHHHHHHHHHHHHHHHHHHHHHHHHHH

Instructions:

1. Set your dashi, and sweet potatoes on in a saucepan over high heat and allow sweet potatoes to become fork tender.

2. Once your potatoes are fork tender, reduce to a low heat, and add in your tofu, and miso paste then stir until your miso dissolve.

3. Add in your remaining ingredients, and allow to cook for another 5 minutes.

4 Serve, and enjoy.

Recipe 11: Black Bean & Tofu Miso Soup

This soup is filling and so tasty you won't want to share.

Yield: 5

Preparation Time: 15 minutes

Ingredient List:

- Dashi (4 cups)
- Black Beans (½ lbs., cooked)
- Tofu (1 lb., extra firm)
- Miso (5 tablespoons, paste)
- Green Onions (2 stalks, finely chopped)

Instructions:

1. Set your dashi on in a saucepan over high heat and allow to come to a boil.

2. While that goes, cut your tofu into ½ inch cubes and add to your dashi pot.

3. Once it begins to boil, reduce to a low heat, and add in your miso paste then stir until your miso dissolve.

4. Add in your onions, and black beans, then remove from the flame.

5. Serve, and enjoy.

Recipe 12: Bacon & Onion Miso Soup

They say everything is better with bacon, and this soup proves that to be true.

Yield: 4

Preparation Time: 15 minutes

Ingredient List:

- Bacon (8 strips, chopped)
- Onion (1, yellow, large, sliced)
- Miso (3 tablespoons, white, paste)
- Dashi (4 cups)
- Green Onions (¼ cup, finely chopped)

HHHHHHHHHHHHHHHHHHHHHHHHHHHHHHHH

Instructions:

1. Set your bacon on to cook in a saucepan over high heat. You want your bacon fat to begin to render from the bacon.

2. Once your fat begins to melt, add in your onions and allow to cook until fragrant (about 2 minutes)

3. Add your dashi, and allow to come to a boil.

4. While that goes, cut your tofu into ½ inch cubes and add to your dashi pot.

5. Once it begins to boil, reduce to a low heat, and add in your miso paste then stir until your miso dissolve.

6. Add in your onions, and remove from the flame.

7. Serve, and enjoy.

Recipe 13: Cabbage & Tomato Miso Soup

This recipe takes simplicity to a whole new level, but though it is simple, it is simply delicious.

Yield: 4

Preparation Time: 15 minutes

Ingredient List:

- Dashi (4 cups)
- Cabbage (1 head, chopped)
- Miso (3 tablespoons, yellow, paste)
- Tomatoes (½ cup, chopped)
- Garlic (2 cloves, minced)

Instructions:

1. Set your dashi on in a saucepan over high heat and allow to come to a boil.

2. Once it begins to boil, reduce to a low heat, and add in your miso paste then stir until your miso dissolve.

3. From this point on you will need to monitor the pot as you do not want your miso paste to boil or reduce as it already has a strong flavor.

4. Add in your remaining ingredients, and allow to cook for another 5 minutes or until cabbage is fork tender.

5. Serve, and enjoy.

Recipe 14: Beefy Miso Soup

If you have never tried beef in a soup, this is a great place to start.

Yield: 4

Preparation Time: 15 minutes

Ingredient List:

- Beef Stock (4 cups)
- Beef Chuck (1 cup., cooked, chopped)
- Miso (3 tablespoons, yellow, paste)
- Green Onions (½ cup, finely chopped)
- Garlic (2 cloves, minced)

Instructions:

1. Set your stock on in a saucepan over high heat and allow to come to a boil.

2. Once it begins to boil, reduce to a low heat, and add in your miso paste then stir until your miso dissolve.

3. Add in your remaining ingredients, and allow to cook for another 5 minutes.

4. Serve, and enjoy.

Recipe 15: Shimeji & Bean Sprout Miso Soup

This bowl of soup will be beautiful to look at, and so tasty you won't want to stop eating it.

Yield: 5

Preparation Time: 15 minutes

Ingredient List:

- Dashi (4 cups)
- Tofu (1 lb., extra firm)
- Miso (5 tablespoons, paste)
- Green Onions (2 stalks, finely chopped)
- Bean Sprouts (2 cups)
- Shimeji Mushrooms (1 cup)

Instructions:

1. Set your dashi on in a saucepan over high heat and allow to come to a boil.

2. While that goes, cut your tofu into ½ inch cubes and add to your dashi pot.

3. Once it begins to boil, reduce to a low heat, and add in your miso paste then stir until your miso dissolve.

4. Stir in your remaining ingredients, and cook for approximately 5 minutes until mushrooms are tender.

5. Serve, and enjoy.

Recipe 16: Salmon Miso Soup

Here is another recipe that continues with the seafood Miso soup trend. It's bound to knock you out your boots.

Yield: 6

Preparation Time: 15 min.

Ingredient List:

- Onion, large, diced (1)
- Carrots, diced (2)
- Celery, diced (3)
- Garlic, finely chopped (4 cloves)
- Kosher salt (1 teaspoon)
- Pepper (½ teaspoons)
- Cinnamon (2 teaspoons)
- Fish broth, low sodium (6 cups)
- Light Miso (2 teaspoons)
- Salmon (1 lb., fillets, sliced)
- Baby Choy (1 bunch, trimmed and chopped)
- Ramen Noodles (½ lb.)

HHHHHHHHHHHHHHHHHHHHHHHHHHHHHHHH

Instructions:

1. Add your vegetables in a saucepan to cook, stirring until fragrant (about 3 minutes) over medium heat.

2. Add your salt, pepper, cinnamon and garlic, and continue to cook for an additional minute.

3. Add broth and miso before bringing to a boil.

4. Now add in your salmon fillets, and reduce to a simmer. Continue until fish is cooked (about 5 - 8 minutes).

5. Stir in ramen noodles, and baby choy to cook for approximately 3 minutes until baby choy is tender.

6. Serve and enjoy!

Recipe 17: Sweet Potato Noodle & Broccoli Miso Soup

Here is a soup that would be perfect for all your vegetarian guests.

Yield: 4

Preparation Time: 15 minutes

Ingredient List:

- Dashi (4 cups)
- Broccoli (2 cups, chopped into florets, blanched)
- Miso (5 tablespoons, paste)
- Ginger (1-inch root, minced)
- Sweet Potato Noodles (2 cups)

Instructions:

1. Set your dashi and ginger on in a saucepan over high heat and allow to come to a boil.

2. Once it begins to boil, reduce to a low heat, and add in your miso paste then stir until your miso dissolve.

3. From this point on you will need to monitor the pot as you do not want your miso paste to boil or reduce as it already has a strong flavor.

4. Add in your broccoli, and noodles, then allow to cook for about 3 – 5 minutes to allow the noodles to heat through.

5. Serve, and enjoy.

Recipe 18: Soy Milk Miso Soup

This is definitely not a traditional miso soup, however if you are a modern twist to your classic miso soup flavors, this is the recipe for you.

Yield: 5

Preparation Time: 15 minutes

Ingredient List:

- Dashi (2 cups)
- Soy Milk (2 cups)
- Tofu (1 lb., extra firm)
- Miso (5 tablespoons, white, paste)
- Mixed Vegetables (1 can, drained and rinsed)

НННННННННННННННННННННННННННННННННН

Instructions:

1. Set your dashi, and soy milk on in a saucepan over high heat and allow to come to a boil.

2. While that goes, cut your tofu into ½ inch cubes and add to your pot.

3. As soon as it begins to boil, reduce to a low heat, and add in your miso paste then stir until your miso dissolve.

4. Add in your vegetables, and allow to cook for about 4 more minutes before removing from the flame.

5. Serve, and enjoy.

Recipe 19: Zoodle Miso Soup

Here is a delicious gluten-free option to your miso soup if you want more than just the broth.

Yield: 4

Preparation Time: 15 minutes

Ingredient List:

- Dashi (4 cups)
- Tofu (1 lb., extra firm)
- Miso (5 tablespoons, paste)
- Green Onions (2 stalks, finely chopped)
- Zoodles (2 cups)

HHHHHHHHHHHHHHHHHHHHHHHHHHHHHHHH

Instructions:

1. Set your dashi on in a saucepan over high heat and allow to come to a boil.

2. While that goes, cut your tofu into ½ inch cubes and add to your dashi pot.

3. Once it begins to boil, reduce to a low heat, and add in your miso paste then stir until your miso dissolve.

4. From this point on you will need to monitor the pot as you do not want your miso paste to boil or reduce as it already has a strong flavor.

5. Add in your onions, and zoodles, then remove from the flame.

6. Serve, and enjoy.

Recipe 20: Shrimp Miso Soup

This homey shrimp miso soup is perfect for a cold winter day.

Yield: 6

Preparation Time: 15 min.

Ingredient List:

- Onion, large, diced (1)
- Carrots, diced (2)
- Celery, diced (3)
- Garlic, finely chopped (4 cloves)
- Kosher salt (1 teaspoon)
- Pepper (½ teaspoons)
- Cinnamon (2 teaspoons)
- Fish broth, low sodium (6 cups)
- Dark Miso (1 tablespoon)
- Shrimp (½ lb., washed and deveined)
- Baby Choy (1 bunch, trimmed and chopped)
- Ramen Noodles (½ lb.)

HHHHHHHHHHHHHHHHHHHHHHHHHHHHHHHH

Instructions:

1. Add your vegetables in a saucepan to cook, stirring until fragrant (about 3 minutes) over medium heat.

2. Add your salt, pepper, cinnamon and garlic, and continue to cook for an additional minute.

3. Add broth and miso before bringing to a boil.

4. Now add in your shrimp fillets, and reduce to a simmer. Continue until fish is cooked (about 5 - 8 minutes).

5. Stir in ramen noodles, and baby choy to cook for approximately 3 minutes until baby choy is tender.

6. Serve and enjoy!

Recipe 21: Beef Udon Miso Soup

Every spoonful of this soup will take you to heaven.

Yield: 4

Preparation Time: 15 minutes

Ingredient List:

- Beef Stock (4 cups)
- Water (1 cup)
- Udon Noodles (2 packs, frozen)
- Shitake Mushroom (½ cup, chopped)
- Shabu Beef (½ lb., cooked, chopped)
- Miso (4 tablespoons, white, paste)
- Togarashi (½ teaspoons)
- Baby bok choy (4 cups, leaves separated)
- Garlic (2 cloves, minced)

HHHHHHHHHHHHHHHHHHHHHHHHHHHHHHHHHH

Instructions:

1. Set your water, and stock on in a saucepan over high heat and allow to come to a boil.

2. Once it begins to boil, reduce to a low heat, and add in your miso paste then stir until your miso dissolve.

3. Add in your remaining ingredients, and allow to cook for another 5 minutes.

4. Serve, and enjoy.

Recipe 22: Collard Green Miso Soup

Create an Asian – Southern fusion with this delicious miso soup.

Yield: 4

Preparation Time: 15 minutes

Ingredient List:

- Vegetable Stock (4 cups)
- Collard greens (1 cup., chopped)
- Miso (3 tablespoons, mild, paste)
- Green Onions (½ cup, finely chopped)
- Garlic (2 cloves, minced)

Instructions:

1. Set your stock on in a saucepan over high heat and allow to come to a boil.

2. Once it begins to boil, reduce to a low heat, and add in your miso paste then stir until your miso dissolve.

3. From this point on you will need to monitor the pot as you do not want your miso paste to boil or reduce as it already has a strong flavor.

4. Add in your remaining ingredients, and allow to cook for another 5 minutes.

5. Serve, and enjoy.

Recipe 23: Shrimp & Lobster Miso Soup

This miso soup gives the ultimate union of shellfish in one bowl.

Yield: 4

Preparation Time: 15 minutes

Ingredient List:

- Dashi (4 cups)
- Lobster meat (1 cup., chopped)
- Miso (3 tablespoons, mild, paste)
- Shrimp (½ lbs., deveined and rinsed)
- Dill (¼ cup, finely chopped)
- Garlic (2 cloves, minced)

HHHHHHHHHHHHHHHHHHHHHHHHHHHHHHHH

Instructions:

1. Set your dashi on in a saucepan over high heat and allow to come to a boil.

2. Once it begins to boil, reduce to a low heat, and add in your miso paste then stir until your miso dissolve.

3. Add in your remaining ingredients, and allow to cook for another 5 minutes.

4. Serve, and enjoy.

Recipe 24: Shitake Mushroom Miso Soup

This soup has a rich shitake flavor and will have you wanting to eat more, and more of it.

Yield: 4

Preparation Time: 15 minutes

Ingredient List:

- Dashi (4 cups)
- Shitake Mushroom (1 cup., chopped)
- Miso (3 tablespoons, mild, paste)
- Green Onions (½ cup, finely chopped)
- Garlic (2 cloves, minced)

HHHHHHHHHHHHHHHHHHHHHHHHHHHHHHHHH

Instructions:

1. Set your dashi on in a saucepan over high heat and allow to come to a boil.

2. Once it begins to boil, reduce to a low heat, and add in your miso paste then stir until your miso dissolve.

3. From this point on you will need to monitor the pot as you do not want your miso paste to boil or reduce as it already has a strong flavor.

4. Add in your remaining ingredients, and allow to cook for another 5 minutes.

5. Serve, and enjoy.

Recipe 25: Salmon & Green Bean Miso Soup

This soup may be simple but it packed a huge punch.

Yield: 4

Preparation Time: 15 minutes

Ingredient List:

- Dashi (4 cups)
- Salmon (1 lb., fillet, grilled, sliced)
- Green Beans (1 cup., blanched, trimmed)
- Miso (3 tablespoons, yellow, paste)
- Garlic (2 cloves, minced)

Instructions:

1. Set your dashi on in a saucepan over high heat and allow to come to a boil.

2. Once it begins to boil, reduce to a low heat, and add in your miso paste then stir until your miso dissolve.

3. Add in your remaining ingredients, and allow to cook for another 3 to 5 minutes to reheat all your ingredients.

4. Serve, and enjoy.

Recipe 26: Turmeric Miso Soup

There are certain spices that are great in soups and turmeric is definitely one of them, when used correctly. Give this soup a try, and see why.

Yield: 5

Preparation Time: 15 minutes

Ingredient List:

- Oil (1 teaspoon)
- Garlic (7 cloves, finely chopped)
- Ginger (1-inch root, peeled and minced)
- Chili (½, seeds removed, diced)
- Carrots (½ cup, shredded)
- Bell Pepper (½, green, thinly sliced)
- Tofu (½ lb., cubed)
- Soy Sauce (2 teaspoons)
- Water (3.5 cups)
- Turmeric (2 teaspoons)
- Apple Cider Vinegar (1 teaspoon)
- Sugar (2 teaspoons)
- Salt (½ teaspoons)
- Black Pepper (½ teaspoons)
- Miso (1 tablespoon, white, paste)
- Green Onions (½ cup, finely chopped)

HHHHHHHHHHHHHHHHHHHHHHHHHHHHHHHHHH

Instructions:

1. Set your oil, garlic, chili and ginger on to cook until fragrant (about a minute) in a saucepan over high heat. Add your water, and allow to come to a boil.

2. While that goes, cut your tofu into ½ inch cubes and add to your dashi pot.

3. Once it begins to boil, reduce to a low heat, and add in your miso paste then stir until your miso dissolve.

4. From this point on you will need to monitor the pot as you do not want your miso paste to boil or reduce as it already has a strong flavor.

5. Add in your onions, and remove from the flame.

6. Serve, and enjoy.

Recipe 27: Adzuki Bean & Vegetable Miso Soup

This soup is tasty and filling.

Yield: 5

Preparation Time: 15 minutes

Ingredient List:

- Dashi (4 cups)
- Adzuki Beans (½ cup., cooked)
- Miso (3 tablespoons, yellow, paste)
- Cauliflower (½ cup, chopped, blanched)
- Carrots (¼ cup, chopped, blanched)
- Green Onions (½ cup, finely chopped)
- Garlic (2 cloves, minced)

Instructions:

1. Set your dashi on in a saucepan over high heat and allow to come to a boil.

2. Once it begins to boil, reduce to a low heat, and add in your miso paste then stir until your miso dissolve.

3. Add in your remaining ingredients, and allow to cook for another 5 minutes.

4. Serve, and enjoy.

Recipe 28: Shrimp & Broccoli Miso Soup

This miso soup is great for pescatarians and meat lovers alike.

Yield: 4

Preparation Time: 15 minutes

Ingredient List:

- Dashi (4 cups)
- Broccoli (1 cup., chopped)
- Miso (3 tablespoons, mild, paste)
- Shrimp (½ lbs., deveined and rinsed)
- Green Onions (½ cup, finely chopped)
- Garlic (2 cloves, minced)

HHHHHHHHHHHHHHHHHHHHHHHHHHHHHHHH

Instructions:

1. Set your dashi on in a saucepan over high heat and allow to come to a boil.

2. Once it begins to boil, reduce to a low heat, and add in your miso paste then stir until your miso dissolve.

3. Add in your remaining ingredients, and allow to cook for another 5 minutes.

4. Serve, and enjoy.

Recipe 29: Chorizo Miso Soup

This delicious recipe creates the perfect breakfast soup.

Yield: 4

Preparation Time: 15 minutes

Ingredient List:

- Dashi (4 cups)
- Chorizo (1 cup., chopped)
- Miso (3 tablespoons, yellow, paste)
- Bean Sprouts (½ cup)
- Garlic (2 cloves, minced)
- Tomatoes (2, wedged)

Instructions:

1. Set your dashi on in a saucepan over high heat and allow to come to a boil.

2. Once it begins to boil, reduce to a low heat, and add in your miso paste then stir until your miso dissolve.

3. Add in your remaining ingredients, and allow to cook for another 5 minutes.

4. Serve & enjoy.

Recipe 30: Lobster Miso Soup

Here we have an elegant recipe for lobster miso soup.

Yield: 6

Preparation Time: 15 min.

Ingredient List:

- Onion, large, diced (1)
- Carrots, diced (2)
- Celery, diced (3)
- Garlic, finely chopped (4 cloves)
- Kosher salt (1 teaspoon)
- Pepper (½ teaspoons)
- Cinnamon (2 teaspoons)
- Fish broth, low sodium (6 cups)
- Light Miso (2 teaspoons)
- Lobster Meat (1lb., chopped)
- Baby Choy (1 bunch, trimmed and chopped)
- Egg Noodles (½ lb., cooked)

HHHHHHHHHHHHHHHHHHHHHHHHHHHHHHHH

Instructions:

1. Add your vegetables in a saucepan to cook, stirring until fragrant (about 3 minutes) over medium heat.

2. Add your salt, pepper, cinnamon and garlic, and continue to cook for an additional minute.

3. Add broth, and miso before bringing to a boil.

4. Now add in your lobster, reduce to a simmer. Continue until lobster is cooked (about 5 - 8 minutes).

5. Stir baby choy and noodles and allow to cook for approximately 3 minutes until baby choy is tender.

6. Serve and enjoy!

About the Author

Jennifer Jones is an accomplished chef, devoted wife and loving mother of two who lives in Boulder, Colorado. As head chef at one of Colorado's most exclusive restaurants, Jennifer's culinary prowess has become legendary and she is often called over to the tables of the rich and famous to accept deep praise for her work.

The beautiful scenery of Boulder is often used as inspiration for some of Jennifer's artistically decorated dishes and the praise is just as much for her creative presentation as the exquisite taste of her food. Her use of greenery to bring out the delectable cuts of meat and fish that adorn the dinner plates is no less than a work of art, and she describes herself as an artist and not a chef.

Jones flourished under the mentorship of her professor at August Escoffier Culinary School of the Arts and went on to study at the Cordon Bleu to perfect her repertoire of international cuisine. While studying abroad, she kept close contact with her mentor from Escoffier, eventually marrying him when she came back to North America.

With all of that culinary ability, you would think some would rub off on the kids? Jennifer's two daughters are both excellent chefs in their own right and have plans to attend Escoffier like their parents. A culinary dynasty, perhaps?

Author's Afterthoughts

With so many books out there to choose from, I want to thank you for choosing this one and taking precious time out of your life to buy and read my work. Readers like you are the reason I take such passion in creating these books.

It is with gratitude and humility that I express how honored I am to become a part of your life and I hope that you take the same pleasure in reading this book as I did in writing it.

Can I ask one small favour? I ask that you write an honest and open review on Amazon of what you thought of the book. This will help other readers make an informed choice on whether to buy this book.

Sincerely,

Jennifer Jones

If you want to be the first to know about news, new books, events and giveaways, subscribe to my newsletter by clicking the link below

https://Jennifer-Jones.gr8.com

or Scan QR-code

Printed in Great Britain
by Amazon